Look at the
graze on this
girl's arm.
What can you
see?

3

It's not what you can see that's important. It's what you can't see. You can't see the **germs**.

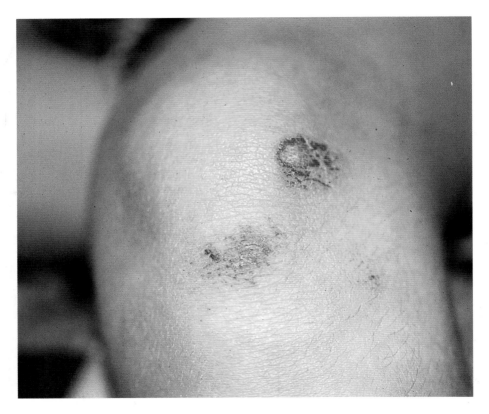

Germs are tiny living things. They can only be seen through a **microscope**.

Germs live everywhere. They live in the
air. They live on the playground. They
live in your home and in your school.

Germs live on your pet. And they live on you. Germs live on just about everything around you.

We touch many dirty things during the day. So lots of germs get on our hands. These germs try to get into our bodies.

Germs wait
for you to
touch your
mouth, nose
or eyes.
Germs can
also get in
through **cuts**
and grazes.

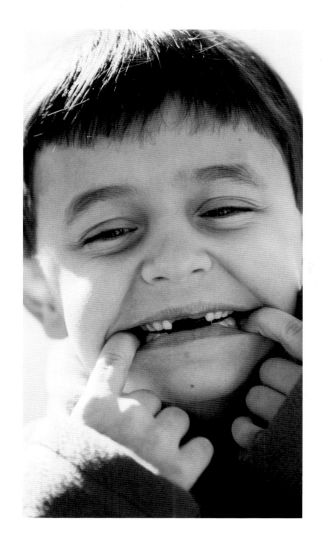

Germs that get into your body begin to
multiply. Soon there are millions of
germs! They attack your body. It tries
to fight the germs.

Your body can kill most germs. Killing germs helps you stay **healthy**.

Your body cannot fight off all germs.
Sometimes germs make you ill.
They can make you sneeze and cough.
They can give you a **fever** and the flu.

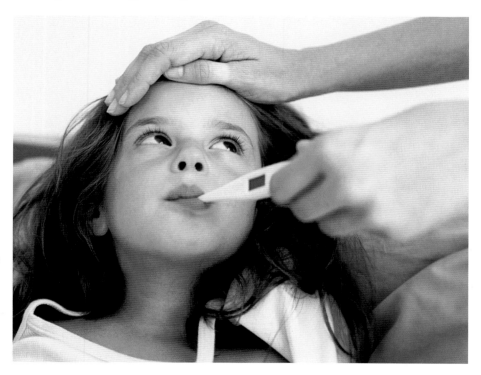

Your doctor might give you some medicine to kill the germs called **bacteria.** Killing these germs will help you to get better.

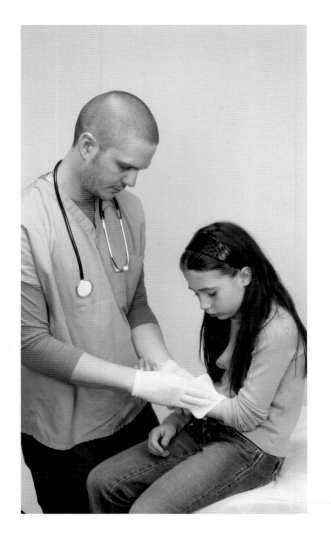

We can get rid of a lot of germs before they get in our bodies. Clean cuts and grazes straight away.

Then cover
them with a
plaster. That
way germs
cannot get in
your body.

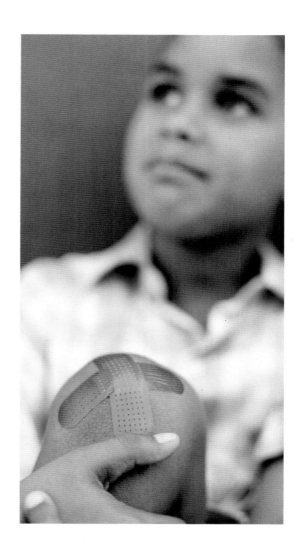

If you cough or sneeze, cover your
mouth and nose with a tissue. This will
stop germs from spreading into the air
or onto your hands.

Washing your hands often during the day will kill lots of germs. Most germs cannot live in warm, soapy water.

Wash your hands after you go to
the toilet.

Wash your hands before you eat.
Don't forget to dry them!

Wash fruit and vegetables before you eat them. This will kill many germs.

Look at this food. It has been sitting on the table all day. What do you think is growing on the food? Germs!

Always put food away as soon as you are finished with it. Make sure you close bags and containers tightly.

Another way to keep germs off food is to put it in the refrigerator. Most germs will die in cold places.

Remember to wash your dishes after using them.

Don't drink out of the same cup that another person has just used. Don't share forks and spoons that have been in your mouth.

Clean the surfaces and floors in your house. Use sponges, cloths and mops. Don't forget the soap or cleaner!

Germs live everywhere. You can keep
most germs away. Keep your body
clean. And don't give germs places
to live.

Facts about Germs

- Not all germs are bad. Our bodies need germs to help break down food. Germs are also used to make cheese and some medicines.

- Antibiotics are medicines made in laboratories. When we are ill these antibiotics can help us get better.

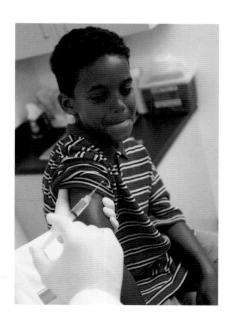

- Antibiotics can only kill germs called bacteria. Bacteria can cause sore throats and earaches.

- Colds and the flu are caused by germs called viruses. Antibiotics cannot kill viruses. Our bodies must fight off viruses by themselves.

- Vaccines are injected medicines made from a small amount of dead or weak germs. These germs help your body fight off some diseases before they make you ill.

Your Body Strikes Back!

■ The best defence against germs is your own body! It has ways of getting rid of germs before they can make you ill.

■ Your skin keeps most germs out.

■ Small hairs in your nose catch the germs that you breathe in. Sneezing makes the germs come out.

■ People don't cry just because they are sad. Tears can wash away dirt, germs and other things that get in your eyes.

■ Millions of germs live in your mouth. Your **saliva** helps to kill many of them.

■ Inside your body are special cells. They destroy the bad germs that get into your body. Without these cells you would be ill all the time.

Books and Websites

Books
Llewellyn, Claire. *How To Stay Healthy* (I Know That!) Franklin Watts Ltd, 2005.

Nelson, Robin. *Staying Clean* Lerner Books, 2008.

Riley, Peter. *Keeping Healthy* (Ways Into Science) Franklin Watts Ltd, 2003.

Rowan, Kate. *I Know How We Fight Germs* (Sam's Science) Walker Books Ltd, 2000.

Senker, Cath. *Keeping Clean* (Health Choices) Hodder Wayland, 2007.

Websites
Welltown
http://www.welltown.gov.uk/home/home_bathmenu.htm

NHS - Juniors first for health
http://www.childrenfirst.nhs.uk/juniors/fun/germzap.html

Glossary

bacteria: germs that can cause sore throats and earaches

cuts: breaks or scratches in the skin

fever: high body temperatures

germs: very small living things that can make people ill

grazes: where you have scraped or scratched the surface of your skin

healthy: fit and well

microscope: a tool that makes very small things appear bigger

multiply: to grow in number

saliva: a liquid you produce in your mouth

Index

Photo Acknowledgements

The photographs in this book appear with the permission of: © Beth Johnson/Independent Picture Service, cover; © Mark Clarke/Photo Researchers, Inc., p 3; © SCF/Visuals Unlimited, p 4; © Richard T. Nowitz/CORBIS, p 5; © PhotoDisc/by Getty Images, pp 6, 28; © Royalty-Free/CORBIS, pp 7, 11; © age fotostock/SuperStock, p 8; © Lisette Le Bon/SuperStock, p 9; © D. Lovegrove/Photo Researchers, Inc., p 10; © Image Source Royalty Free Images, pp 12, 15, 17; © Tom & Dee Ann McCarthy/CORBIS, p 13; © Todd Strand/Independent Picture Service, pp 14, 21, 25, 26; © LWA-Stephen Welstead/CORBIS, p 16; © Image Source/SuperStock, p 18; © Brendan Curran/Independent Picture Service, pp 19, 22; © Andrew Bret Wallis/SuperStock, p 20; © Purestock/SuperStock, p 23; © Norbert Schaefer/CORBIS, p 24; © BAUMGARTNER OLIVIA/CORBIS SYGMA, p 27.